Smilemusic
Publications

Australia

Copyright © 2023 Emma Louise Drew

ISBN: 978-0-6459741-0-2

ACT, Australia
www.emmadrew.mymusicstaff.com
http://www.youtube.com/@emsmusic3414
Please contact emsmusic@yahoo.com

ABN 64 514673740

Smilemusic Publications is an imprint under the publication name of Emma Louise Drew.

*This book is dedicated to
all my students
who bring beauty to the world
everyday through their music.*

15 Beginner Piano Pieces

Emma Drew

Songs To Smile About

Smilemusic
Publications

Australia

Table of Contents

About this Collection

This compilation of songs provides performance repertoire in a variety of styles with varying degrees of difficulty for the beginner student to explore and grow in their reading and technical skills. Suggested fingering can be adjusted to suit the individual to best support the flow of the music. I encourage the performer to embrace the theme of each song bringing out the individual character of each piece. I hope you enjoy learning and performing these songs and that they bring a smile to you and your listeners.

(You can listen to the pieces on YouTube @emsmusic3414)

About the Composer

Emma Drew is a piano/vocal instructor, composer, recording artist, accompanist, and choir master. In addition to running a thriving music tuition studio, she has released the single 'Torn' and album '...With a Cup of Tea,' which can be accessed through all major streaming outlets. For further publications of Emma Drew, please visit Sheet Music Direct or Sheet Music Plus.

Emma was immersed in music from a young age, becoming proficient in singing, piano, trumpet, violin, and acoustic and bass guitar. She started composing at the age of fourteen and commenced teaching instrumental lessons from the age of 17. Emma has been involved in many bands (brass, stage, and concert), string ensembles, orchestras, vocal groups, and pop bands.

Emma's passion to enhance the lives of people around her has been her driving force behind her compositions and teaching. Emma believes and teaches that music is a gift - not to the performer but from the performer to the listener, in order to bring beauty to the lives of others.

Upto Mischief

Emma Drew

Allegro

Popsicle

Emma Drew

Steady Rock

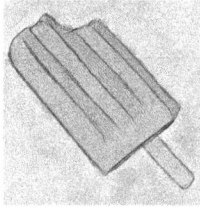

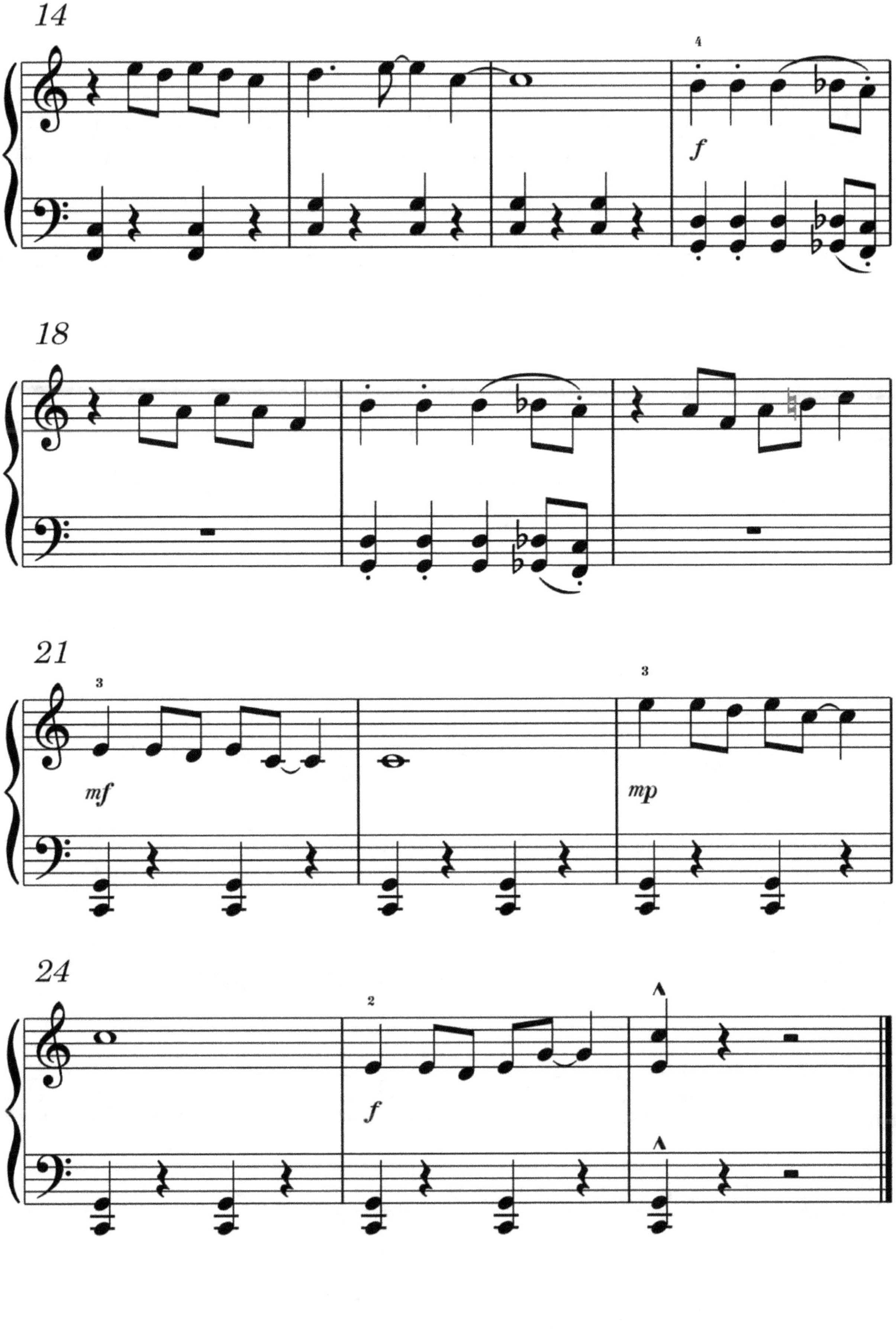
14
4
f
18
21
3
mf
3
mp
24
2
f

Race Car Rally

Emma Drew

Driving Quickly

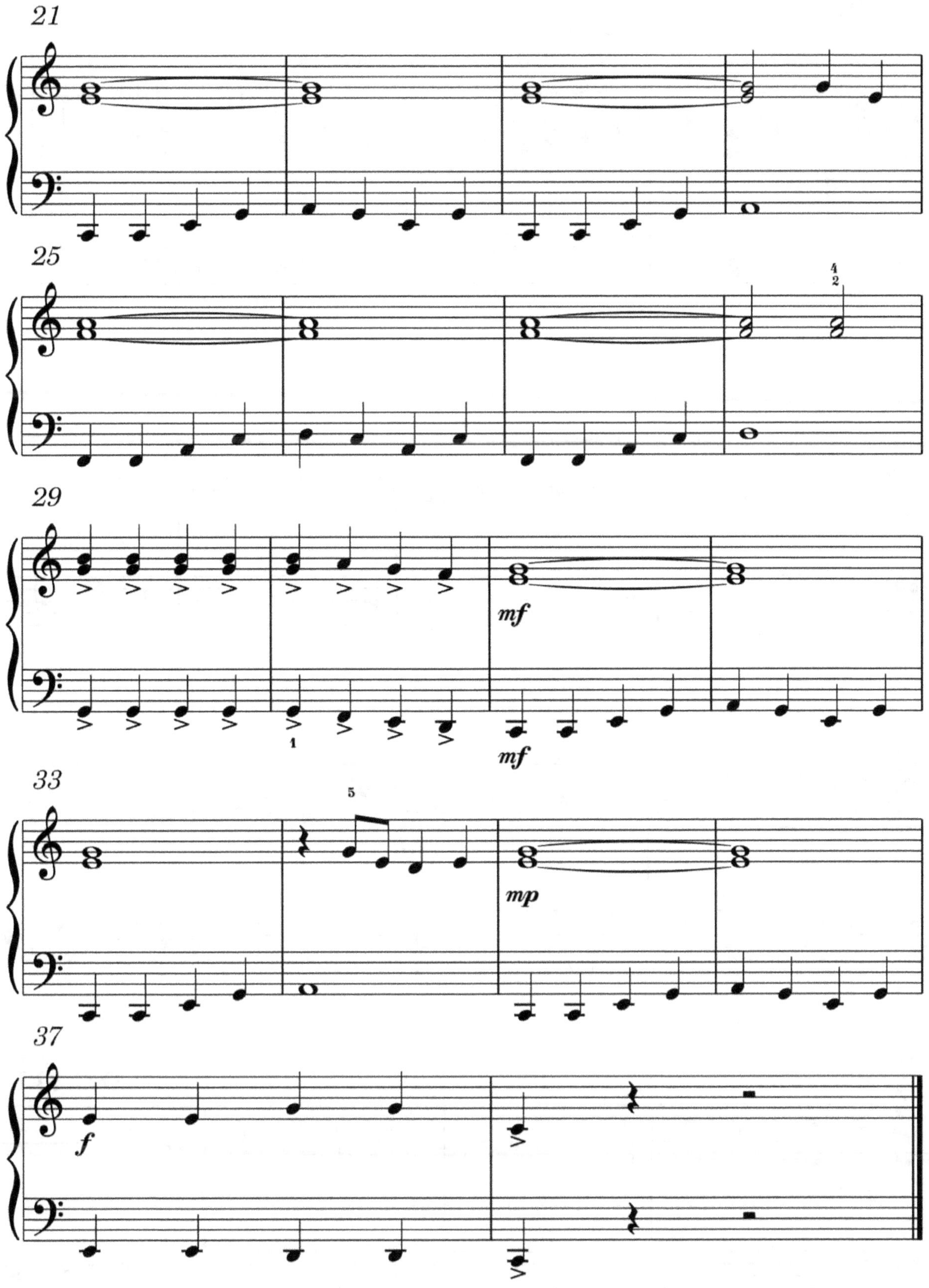
21
25
29
mf
mf
33
mp
37
f

Summer Joy

Emma Drew

Windy Days

Emma Drew

15

Happy Vibes

Emma Drew

Allegretto

Cantabile, a la Mozart

13
2
16
Ritard.
19
A trottin' moderato, swing
mf
22
2
25
2
5
1
Ritard.

The River

Emma Drew

Allegretto

espressivo

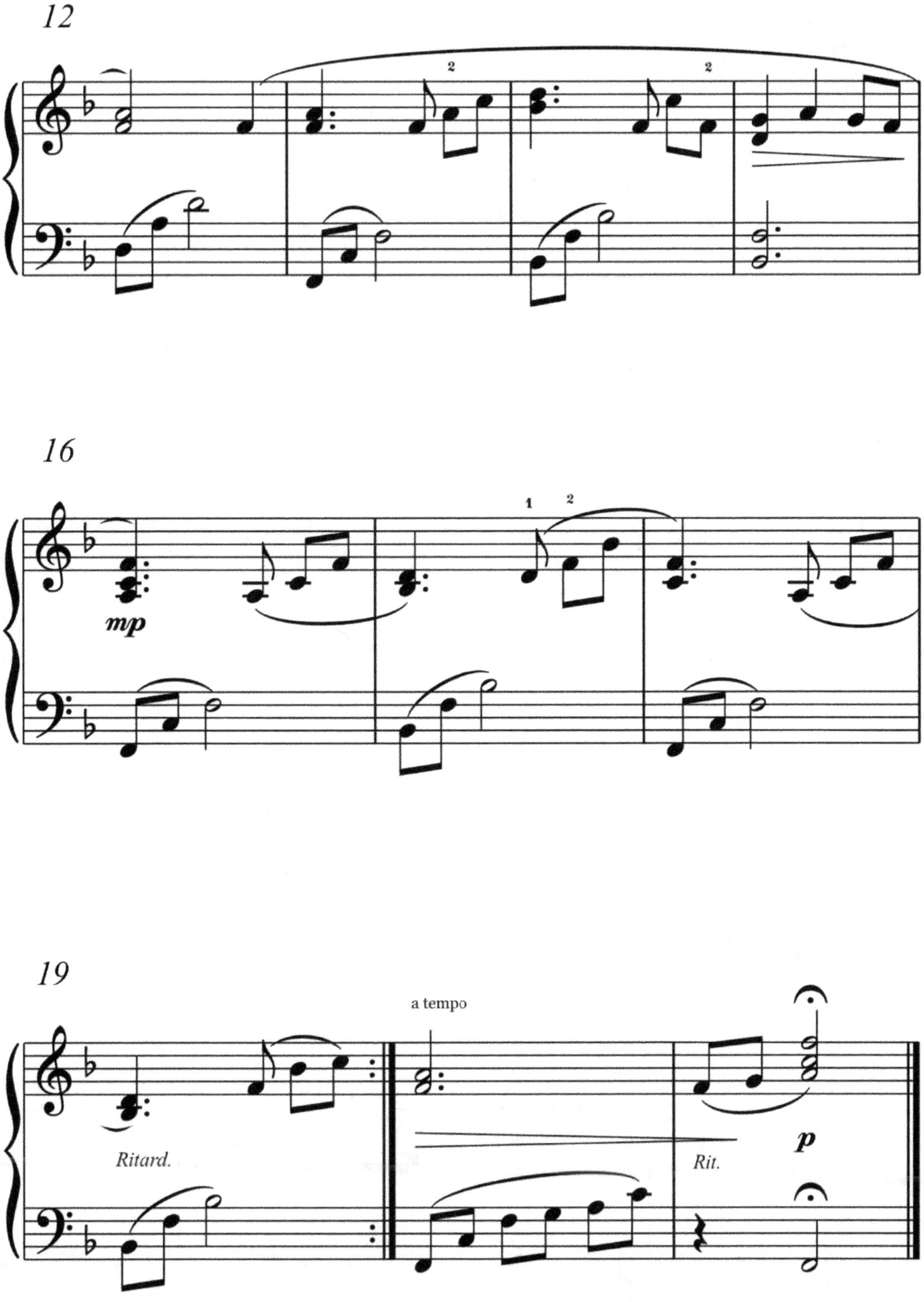
12
16
mp
19
a tempo
Ritard.
Rit.
p

Groovin' Along

Emma Drew

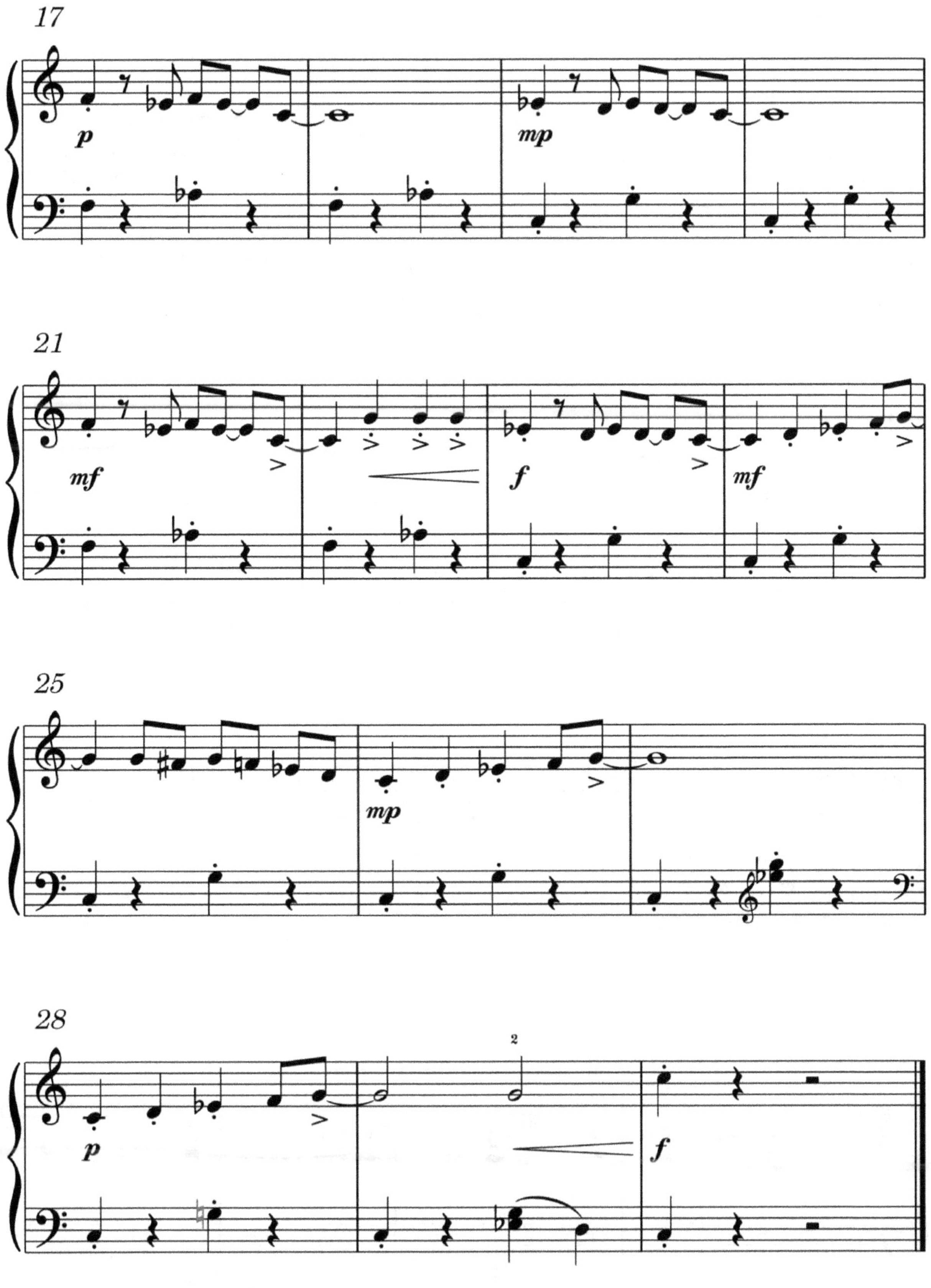
17
p
mp
21
mf
f
mf
25
mp
28
p
2
f

Camelot

Emma Drew

Majestic

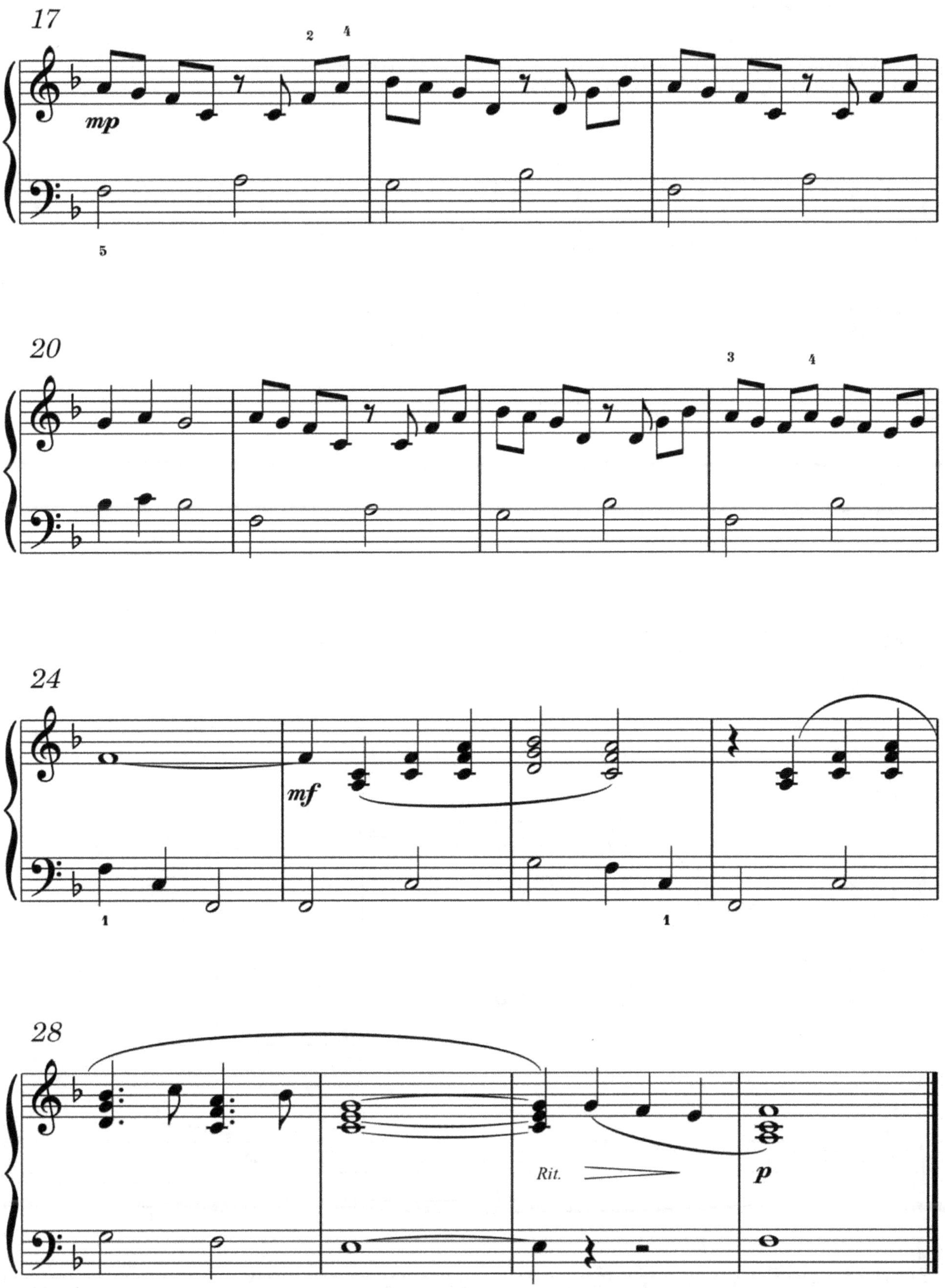
17
mp
20
24
mf
28
Rit.
p

I Dream ...

Emma Drew

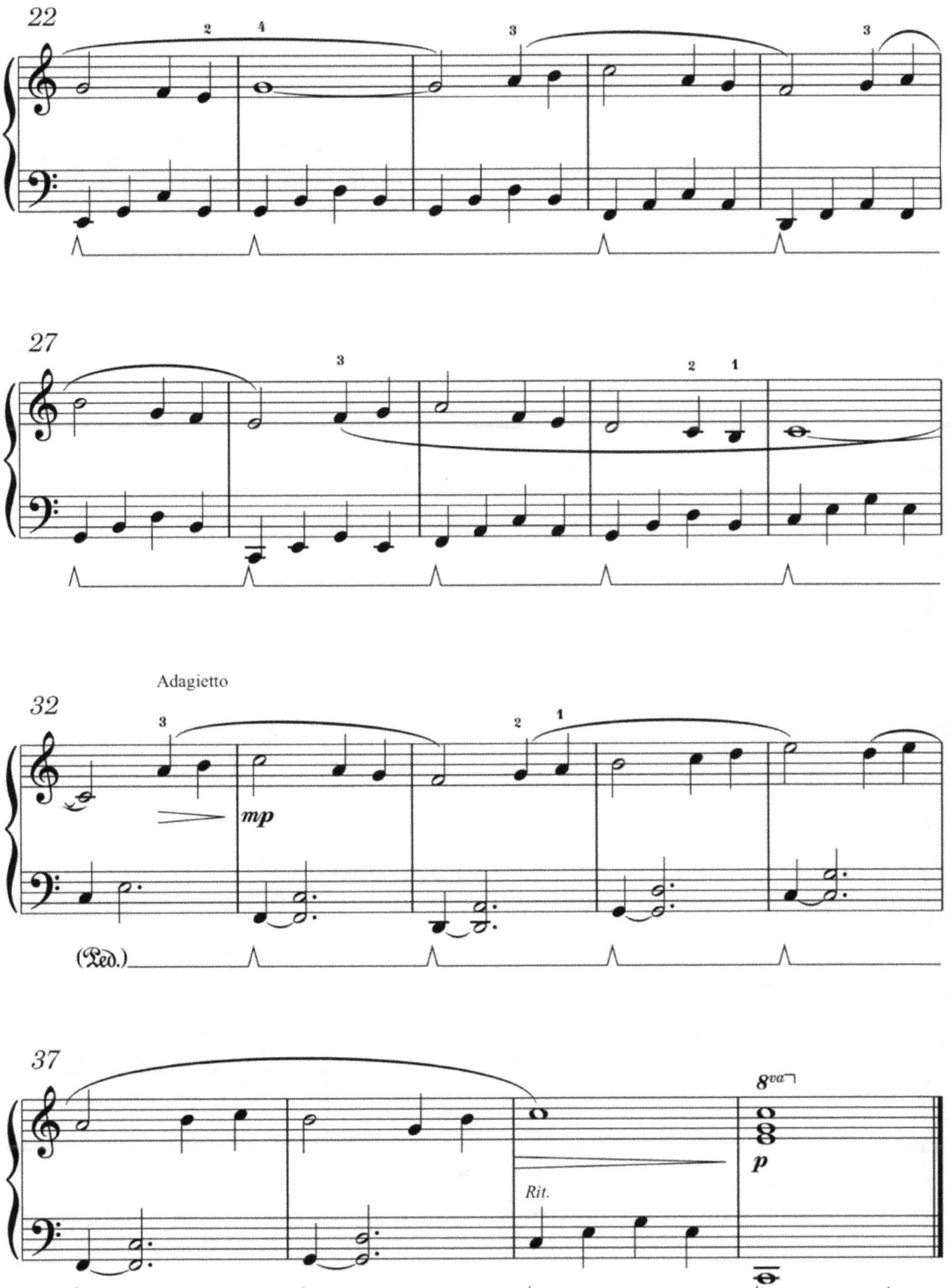
22
27
Adagietto
32
mp
(Ped.)
37
8va
p
Rit.

Sun Shower

Emma Drew

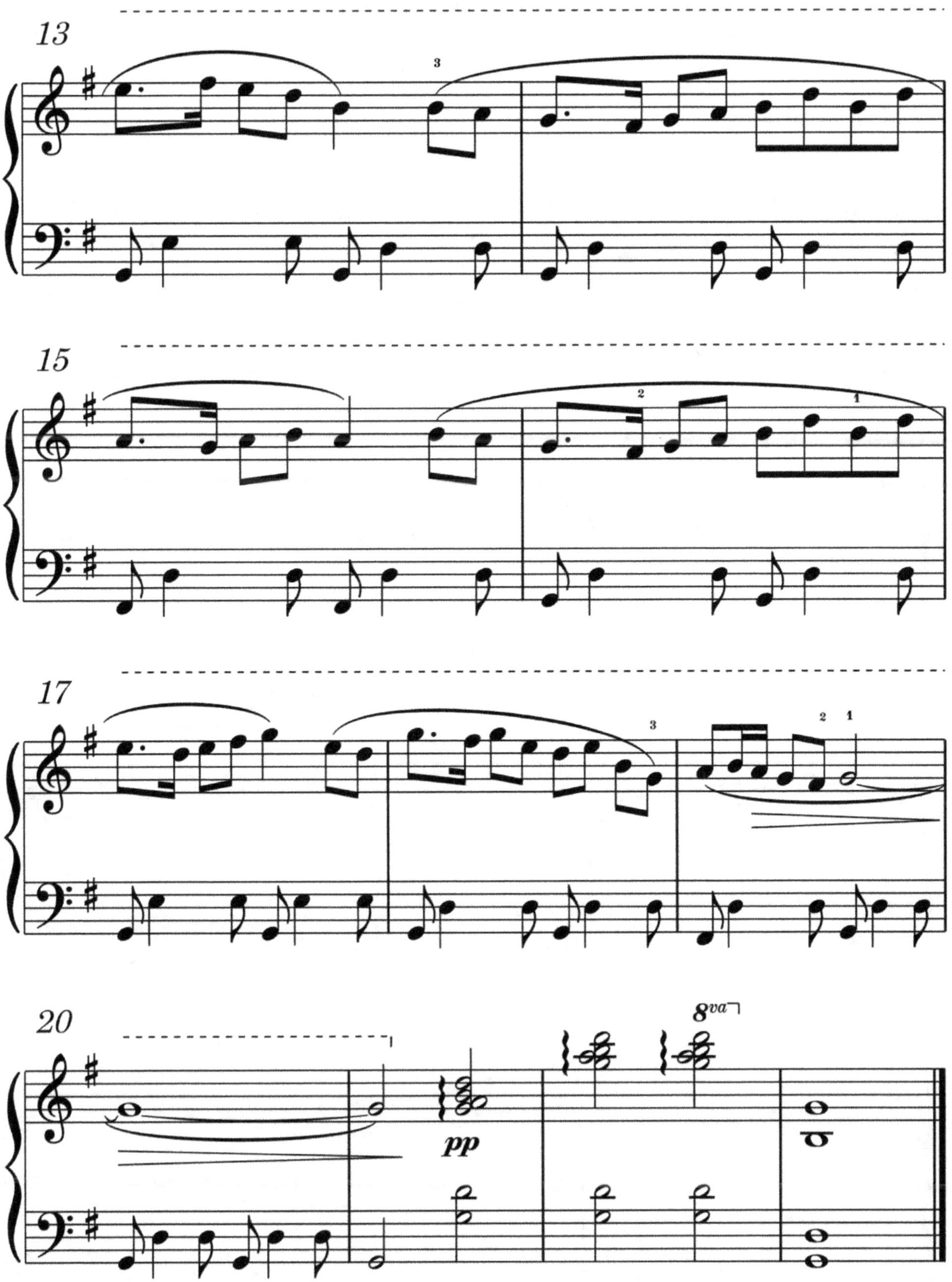
13
3
15
2
1
17
3
2 1
20
8va
pp

As Darkness Falls

Emma Drew

Mysteriously

Waterfall

Emma Drew